POCKET IMAGES

Bury

POCKET IMAGES

Bury

John Hudson

NONSUCH

First published 1993
This new pocket edition 2007
Images unchanged from first edition

Nonsuch Publishing
Cirencester Road, Chalford
Stroud, Gloucestershire, GL6 8PE
www.nonsuch-publishing.com

Nonsuch Publishing is an imprint of NPI Media Group

British Library Cataloguing in Publication Data.
A catalogue record for this book is available from the British Library.

ISBN 978-1-84588-409-3

Typesetting and origination by NPI Media Group
Printed in Great Britain

Contents

Introduction

In recent times Bury has often enjoyed the reputation of a political see-saw, tending to vote for whichever party comes to power. That encourages seekers after truth from the TV companies and the national newspapers to come trekking north every five years, booking into the most expensive hotel in Manchester and then venturing forth up Bury New Road to discover how Britain will be voting the next time around.

Passing the boundary sign at Prestwich, they usually end up telling the nation that Bury is a kind of long, thin place with no real heart. Readers can be reassured that the Bury of this book is far from long and thin, and its heart lies where it always has, in a mile's radius of the market-place. I have no real axe to grind any more about the local government changes of 1974; thirty-plus years ago, after all, is distant enough even to qualify for inclusion in these pages. But I think I know Bury people well enough to realize that when they buy a book on the town they do not have Sheepfoot Lane, Prestwich, Higher Lane, Whitefield or Stand Lane, Radcliffe in mind.

This, then, is the Bury of our childhood if our memories go back to the end of the Second World War or beyond—the Bury of our parents and our grandparents. It was a tight-knit world of terraced houses, busy shopping streets, cotton mills, paper works and slipper factories, all belching smoke and blazing with light on grey winter evenings. It was a good job it was a tight-knit world, for the only time you could see beyond the edge of town to the moors was towards the end of Wakes Week, when suddenly Holcombe Hill and its green and brown brothers reappeared to surround us for a day or two like big, friendly giants.

To many, Bury, with a population of 60,000 in 1938, was always just the right size for a place—or just the wrong size if you happened to dislike small towns. It was big enough to have something of most things, but rarely to excess. It meant that, if you were happy with superb and cheap everyday shopping amenities, a picture house for every day of the week, work close at hand and a football team that allowed you a glimpse of good second division sides like West Ham, Spurs and Sheffield Wednesday a few times a season, you had no problems. The trouble only started when you began casting envious glances at Market Street, Manchester, the Ardwick Hippodrome, Manchester United and Bolton Wanderers.

For the purposes of this book those outside influences might scarcely have existed. This is the Bury of the past in sharp focus—its pubs, coffee rooms and oyster houses, its chapels, churches and meeting rooms. In my choice of photographs I have tried hard to concentrate on human interest, and fear I might occasionally have offended would-be contributors in doing so. What I have endeavoured to do is avoid good 1893 views of buildings that look like bad 1993 ones. It matters little to me if a shot shows the church tower before the ivy was cut away, or the mill before the 1926 extension was built. Give me the 1920s dance band, the demon hockey girls, the man pushing the Sunlight Soap tricycle ...

Where outside influences did creep into the town, it was usually to its greater prosperity. Being so close to Manchester, it was unquestionably lucky in having a diversity of industries that ensured that it was not wholly dependent on cotton—paper, engineering, slippers, confectionery and furniture all had their part to play. Then there were the Lancashire Fusiliers at Wellington Barracks, a factor that always kept Bury in the mind of the county hierarchy and gave the town a good show other than the Whit Walks to watch once a year. The down side, of course, and one that was evident when it came to recruiting for the Second World War with the scars of Gallipoli scarcely healed from the First, was that, while the Fusiliers looked splendid marching down the Rock on church parade, rather fewer of them than had set out tended to return to their mums and girlfriends from foreign fields.

So do we regret the passing of the days relived with affection in these pages? I think that if we are honest with ourselves, we do not. What would the Edwardians have given for our warm homes, our shopping centre, our mobility? If we fail to capitalize on these advantages, to run the risk of even contemplating the thought that society at that time was inherently happier than it is today, then that is our fault, not the result of the way the world has turned out.

Such thoughts should not lessen our enjoyment of looking back, and wishing, in a vain and wistful way, that we could melt into the scenes that we recognize on these pages. Some, doubtless, would long to be in thronging Union Square for some pre-war Whit Walks, others on the back row of the Star Cinema on a warm summer night. I confess in the book that, if I could play that magical game, I would for some inexplicable reason step right back into page 95, stroll along Haymarket Street to the UCP café on the corner and order the biggest plate of steak and cowheels on the menu. I'd probably regret it as soon as I did so, and immediately curse myself for not allowing my fantasies-come-true to extend to Julia Roberts, or the Shakers beating Manchester United 8-0 in the FA Cup at Wembley—to heck with steak and cowheels. But before I did so I'd live and breathe every sight and sound of that Haymarket Street walk, because it is little home-town streets like these that have made us the way we are, and it is as well that we recognize this.

Perhaps what we miss most of all in our modern life is stability, but was life any more stable then? Tell that to the lads at Gallipoli, the 1920s dole queues, the proprietors of one-time haunts of pillars of local society like the Derby Hotel and Coffee Rooms, and the owners of any number of big old suburban mansions, now all gone. Because the images shown here are captured forever, fleeting moments held in time, it does not mean that the life they show was any more serene or predictable than ours. Seconds after the photographer had pressed the shutter the subjects of his picture were on their way—to miss their bus, stub their toe, burn the tea and do all the things that we do and wish we didn't. Perhaps they're all out there somewhere now, those forefathers of ours, looking down laughing at us and longing to sample our world of pizzas and Broadband, just as fervently as I'd like to step into page 95.

John Hudson,

One

Along the Rock

Two buildings dominate this aerial view of the Market Place taken between the wars: the parish church and, beyond it on the other side of the Wylde, the Drill Hall, still standing today, in Castle Street. Fleet Street, running alongside the church and off the bottom right of the picture, was the beginning of Bury's main shopping thoroughfare, changing its name as it progressed north-eastwards to Rock Street, Stanley Street and finally Water Street. All of this caused confusion, and when Hornby Buildings were put up to become a focal point of Rock Street in 1935, the opportunity was taken to rename all four streets the Rock. It was not until after the Second World War that local people began to feel fully at ease with the change, and for years other Lancashire towns teased Bury mercilessly for coming up with such a dashing name for its high street. It was not until 1956, with Elvis Presley putting rock in the headlines throughout the world, that the name change came to be seen as an act of unconscious marketing genius.

Looking down Fleet Street from the Market Place, 1903. The statue to Sir Robert Peel, Bury's most famous son, is black with grime, and a street vendor's cart in front of it advertises sandwiches. Beyond the parish church the Old Bank building is occupied by the printers Fletcher and Speight, who previously had premises in Silver Street and published the Bury Monthly Visitor, as well as cricket and football handbooks for clubs all over the north and the Midlands.

Bury parish church as it was in 1871, with a Perpendicular tower built in the 1840s attached to a simple Georgian building dating from 1780. It appears that it was the tower's lot in life never to be to scale with its adjoining church—patently too large for the 1780 building and too small for the present one, which was opened in 1876. By 1871 the bronze statue of Peel was twenty years old, but its plinth still looks remarkably pristine.

Above: Numbers 46–52 Fleet Street, 1884, shortly before these mean little buildings, on what by then was a prime town centre site, were demolished to make way for premises more in keeping with late Victorian times. Both Barlow's–'The People's Hat And Cap Mart'–and Briggs the drapers–'Goods At Cost Price And Less'–make much of the bargains to be had in their closing-down sales.

Opposite below: The 1780s parish church in the course of demolition, less than a century after its construction. Its woodwork was said to be in a state of dangerous decay and the rector, Canon E.J.G. Hornby, declared in 1871 that during the twenty-one years of his incumbency his parishioners had been condemned to worship in a building that most employers would not have used as a loomshed for their workpeople. The architect for the new church was J.S. Crowther, a Gothic revivalist then busy with the restoration of Manchester Cathedral, but there were those who said that the church's true designers were the medieval builders of Tintern Abbey in the Wye Valley, to which its nave bears an uncanny resemblance.

Above and left: Memories of Norman Willis, above and below right, who dealt in wools, hosiery and the like at 45 Fleet Street before his retirement in 1925. The shop was opened by his father, James Willis, in 1880.

Peter Hardman's fish and game shop and oyster house had been at 30 and 32 Fleet Street for only three years when this picture was taken of the premises in their 1887 Golden Jubilee finery, but the popular Mr Hardman was well established as the leader of his field in Bury. The heroes he commemorates on his placard are 'Real English Natives'—surely not a slighting reference to the Queen's German descent? They include ex-Mayor Burrow on the left and Mayor Horridge. Since his oyster rooms were well frequented by local worthies, it could be that Mr Hardman was trying to butter up his customers. The oyster depot, on the left of the picture, was converted from a room that formerly housed a public weighing machine, with 'handsome supper-room in the rear furnished with marble tables, and every requisite in first-class style'. Even in 1890 you could telephone and book a table, on Bury 27.

Bury.   Fleet Street.

16

Downham's still catches the eye on the corner of Union Street in 1958, and farther up the Rock there are such familiar local names as Read Franklin and Heywood's music shop, and Bostock's shoes. By now, though, national chain stores and shops are beginning to dominate the heart of Bury's shopping street—and who, in 1958, would have believed that in a handful of years' time the pendulum would be swinging again, with the new shopping centre switching the focus away from the Rock?

Opposite above: It's summer 1910 and Jack Holland's sports shop window is full of cricket bats and tennis racquets for the short season. Stores like Greenhalgh's confectioners and Benton's tobacconists are a reminder that shops serving both specialist and everyday needs rubbed shoulders in the high streets of Edwardian Britain. Second from the right, at number 22, is Lepp's jewellers, formerly Waldvogel's, where thousands of local couples bought their engagement and wedding rings.

Opposite below: Fleet Street in Edwardian times, looking towards Rock Street. On the left the shops include Hewart's the drapers and milliners, and a branch of the Lipton food chain. Hewart's was founded in 1867 and by 1890 the business had forty workers in its dress department, turning out a thousand gowns a year. The scene on the right, at the corner of Union Street, is dominated by Downham's ironmongery. Founded in 1853, the business merged with John Kay and Sons in 1969 and the building was demolished two years later.

Above: A scene of dilapidation: Rock Street from the corner of Eden Street in the 1880s.

The brave new face of shopping in Bury in the late 1930s: Clegg's furnishers boasted forty modern showrooms.

Opposite above: Rock Street at its junction with Clough Street, which led into Rochdale Road, in 1910. These are the old properties that were cleared for the Hornby Buildings, which were set back from the road in the 1930s. It was a complicated process, which at one time saw the shops trading as normal while their rear rooms were being demolished to make way for the new block, into which many of them eventually moved. There was no future, however, for the Roe Buck Hotel, now simply numbered as one of Bury's scores of forgotten inns.

Numbers 8–16 Stanley Street, just beyond Clough Street at its junction with Butcher Lane, c. 1900. On the right, Kay's the brushmakers advertise their wares in time-honoured style, while the Eagle and Child is flanked by two tobacconists, Smith's and Wilkins's.

Water Street, 1890s. Calling itself the Manchester Mourning Warehouse, Robinson's at number 14 presents a cheerless picture, and it was not long before the shop changed its image. By the 1890s Bury folk were not quite so preoccupied with the constant threat of mortality and the struggle for survival as they had been a generation or two previously, and the advertisement for Robinson's, seen in Bolton Street on page 107, tells a very different story from 'Mourning Orders Completed With Despatch'. Even here there appear to be brightly coloured boas in the window.

After Water Street, even the name change of 1935 did not affect this far-flung end of the Rock at Moorside. The first electric tram, shown here, ran from Jericho to Moorside in 1903. Businesses from right to left are the Foresters Arms, the Moorgate branch of the Bury Coffee House, whose more popular venue was in Market Street, the Swan Hotel, Robinson's ladies' outfitters at number 21—across the street from the firm's Mourning Warehouse, pictured above—and Wynn's Stores.

Two

Working Lives

Mastermind of the rebuilding of the parish church in the 1870s was Canon Edward James Geoffrey Hornby, incumbent from 1850 to 1888 in succession to his father, who took office in 1818. The Hornbys were related to and brought in to the living by the Earls of Derby. The younger one, following a familiar pattern among the well-connected, was the third son who went into the Church. Lest this gives the impression that he was a weak and ineffective time-server, such thoughts should be dismissed. Outspoken and strong-willed, he was long remembered as a man who feared God and absolutely no one else.

Another century and another Hornby as Rector of Bury, this one Hugh Leycester, who served long and well from 1930 to 1953. Tall and patrician, he had the added kudos of being related to A.N. Hornby, the swashbuckling Lancashire batsman immortalized in Francis Thompson's haunting poem, At Lord's: 'O my Hornby and my Barlow long ago'.

There seems something oddly staged about this picture of W.E.S. Richmond's veterinary surgery in Knowlsey Street, but any cameraman working with animals in the less than Instamatic world of 1913 probably needed all the help he could get. It is very likely that this picture was taken to mark Mr Richmond's recent move from Silver Street. He must have been a busy man, for the whole of horse-drawn Bury was served by just five vets' surgeries at this time.

Only the fact that the vehicle is not a police car but a fire engine tells us that this is not a picture of the Keystone Kops in action. The scene is close to the old fire station in Stanley Street, very near to the site of the present station. There have been fire engines in Bury for at least two hundred years, but the first motor vehicle, made by Leyland, was bought in 1913. Among interested onlookers in front of Holt's tobacconists is, on the left, a woman dressed in the type of clogs and shawl that survived among mill workers up until the First World War.

Doffers, Warth Mill, c. 1906.

Above: Bolton Street Railway Station, pre-1923, when the Lancashire and Yorkshire Railway was grouped with the LMS and the station headboards were changed accordingly. The original terminal for the electric service to Manchester, the station is now the home of the East Lancashire Railway.

One of the English Electric five-coach trains that plied the line between Manchester Victoria and Bury Bolton Street from 1915 to 1959, powered by side contact to a third rail. The train here is in pre-1923 LYR livery, and most who used the service before the smart new green models were introduced in 1959 will remember the veteran carriages looking a great deal more scruffy than this. The second coach was first class, which seemed an anomaly in the train's later years. A friend of the compiler still talks of meeting an acquaintance on Bolton Street Station, chatting cheerfully with him, and then each going his separate way—first and third class—for the couple of minutes' ride to Radcliffe.

Opposite below: Sixteen staff members line up for a Bolton Street Station group photograph of the early 1920s, many of them with the bearing of the soldiers they had doubtless been just a few years before.

Paper workers at Olive's Woolfold Mill in Edwardian times. The paper industry was one of Bury's biggest employers after textiles, with Elton Paper Mills and James Wrigley and Sons at Bridge Hall enjoying an international reputation.

Opposite above: Wilson and Stockall, with workshops off Union Square and showrooms in the Market Place, made ambulances from 1877, and even claimed the first patent for such vehicles. This horse-drawn two-deck accident ambulance included a cunning lifting device to raise the first patient up towards the roof, but one can imagine the ride being somewhat precarious as the ambulance rattled over the cobblestones. The firm was keen on inventive devices such as this, even coming up with a steel tyre built to keep the wheel out of tram lines. The firm, which also specialized in 'medical gigs' for doctors and quickly turned to motor ambulances at the turn of the century, ceased trading in 1961.

Opposite below: Dennis of Guildford produced this splendid vehicle for Bury Corporation in around 1930, and had the foresight to photograph it before it had been tainted by northern muck.

Workers at Warth Mills, 1953. The bunting is doubtless for the Coronation.

The streets of Bury were thronged with some peculiar looking vehicles at the turn of the century, and in 1895 nobody spared a second thought for this two-man delivery tricycle.

Shop floor workers and management stand proudly by a modern press at Joseph Webb and Sons' Irwell Forge, Elton, in the 1920s. Webb's, founded in 1846, was a major employer by the early years of the twentieth century, stocking iron and steel in bulk, and supplying industry and the armed forces with a vast range of machine parts.

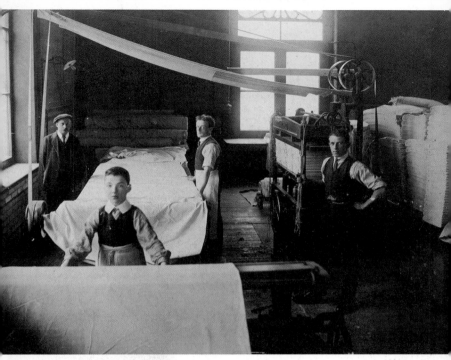

The warehouse of Pearson and Co.'s Moorside Mill in Barlow Street, at around the end of the First World War. The mill has been demolished.

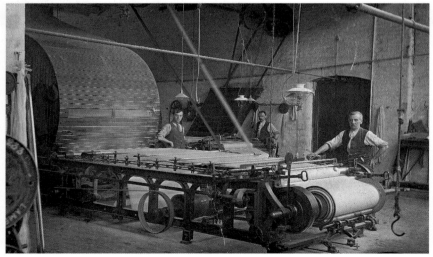

The first electric tram in Bury ran between Moorside and Jericho in 1903, and is pictured on page 20. A dozen years later, in 1915, one of the last sections of track was being laid, along Walmersley Road from Limefield to the New Inn in Walmersley.

Opposite above: Handloom weavers' cottages, known as Chesham Place at Huntley Brook, on Rochdale Old Road, with their well-lit loomsheds on the third floor. They survived for a couple of decades after the Second World War, and their eventual demolition raised searching questions about official attitudes towards the preservation of our industrial heritage.

Opposite below: Slaching machine, Victoria Mill, c. 1900.

If it wasn't cotton, paper or engineering that supported you and your family in Bury in the early years of the twentieth century, then the chances were that it was slippers. These pictures, the first (above) from the end of the First World War and the other (opposite) from a few years earlier, show life at J.H. Parker's Greenbrook Factory at Chesham. Founded with just twenty workers in 1905, it could turn out 24,000 pairs of slippers at its peak, and was also popular for its children's sandals. Like cotton, the slipper industry was labour intensive for both men and women: above is the lasting room, with the wooden lasts prominent on the right; opposite is a vast roomful of operatives in the stitching department, taking a brief break for the camera. Their products, in the foreground, do not look vastly different from the slippers favoured by many people today, some hundred years on.

The carriers' carts were a lifeline to the villages, but they buzzed busily around the town centre, too, at the turn of the century. Sutton and Co.'s vehicles were a familiar sight, albeit not always with a handsome young woman sitting on the shafts.

Suddenly, in 1960, motor cars are available in any colour as long as they are black. This is Auty and Lees' showroom on the Rock, where the new Vauxhall Victor rubs shoulders with a long-standing favourite—the neat and compact Bedford van. The latter looks a decent buy at £585, but the dreaded purchase tax—the 1950s and early 1960s answer to VAT—added a further £117 to that price.

Three

High Days and Holidays

Harvest Festival at Brunswick Methodist Church on North Street, which, even when not dressed with the fruits of the earth, belied the Nonconformists' supposed preference for simple and austere places of worship. Its history stemmed from a breakaway group from Union Street Chapel in the 1830s, the church seen here opening in 1864. It lasted barely more than a hundred years, until 1968. When it was demolished, as with the weavers' cottages on page 34, there were many who believed that post-war Britain was moving too far and too fast in sweeping away its heritage.

Opposite above: A queue for the TV show 'The Good Old Days'? Not quite. This is the scene at the Brunswick Methodist Whit Walks in 1907, the young women's sumptuous hats again reminding us that Nonconformists could be as flamboyant as any other citizens.

Opposite below: The laying of the foundation stone at the Art Gallery in 1900, one of a number of significant municipal buildings opened in Bury at the turn of the century. Built by the local company Thompson and Brierley, whose cranes are prominent around the platform, the Art Gallery was opened in October of the following year by Lord Derby.

The Bury Coffee House and Central Dining Rooms in Market Street were the chief of four branches in the town, the others being in Moorgate (see page 20), Rochdale Road and Crostons Road, Elton. They opened at 5.00 a.m. and worked through until 10.00 p.m., six days a week, and one of their several dining rooms was for ladies only. 'All who wish to witness an animated scene should visit these rooms about noon any day in the week, when the numerous patrons of the house avail themselves of the opportunity of tasting the excellent dinner placed on the table at fourpence to eightpence apiece,' a guide for 1890 reported. This picture, a dozen years later in 1902, shows the rooms celebrating the coronation of Edward VII.

The year must be around the time when the Suffragette movement was launched, in 1906, for two of these women from Blackford Bridge Congregational Church wear Votes For Women sashes. From the fancy dress of the others, however, and the suitcases with the message 'Trip To Blackpool' displayed prominently, it seems likely that they had been taking part in a political skit, rather than spreading the Pankhursts' word in earnest.

A well-known image to those who love Bury and its history. What stirring pageantry there was when the Lancashire Fusiliers' South African War memorial was unveiled in the Market Place, upstaging for a while the statue of Sir Robert Peel. The artist was George Frampton, best known for his Peter Pan in Kensington Gardens, and the unveiling was by the Lord Lieutenant of Lancashire, Lord Derby. The statue increasingly became a traffic hazard as the petrol engine revolutionized the town centre streets, and it was removed to Whitehead Gardens in the 1920s. It stands there today, a splendidly vivid work still in fine condition.

After the unveiling, another famous Bury photo opportunity: an old folks' treat in the Drill Hall, attended by the Mayor, Alderman Butcher and the town's youngest ever Mayoress, his nine-year-old daughter. The whole proceedings have been brought to a halt for this single still photograph—odd to think that today a get-together of this size would be recorded by a score of video cameras, and viewed in moving colour on the TV screen the same evening.

Not roasted on the bonfire but over charcoal at the fairground, chillingly close to the Knowsley Street abattoirs, the coronation ox also added to the festivities of 1911, though he looks none too cheerful about the prospect here. Weighing in at 700 lb, he was the gift of Councillor Albert Taylor's wife. Councillor Taylor is on the right with the organizing committee. Were organizers of events as frivolous as an ox roast really so sombre and self-important as these men appear, or are they being sold short by the convention of the time not to smile for the camera? Perhaps, deep down, they were just feeling sorry for the poor old ox.

Opposite: The coronation bonfire, June 1911. Wicker skips were everywhere around the cotton mills, and it seems that most of them went up in smoke that summer.

Above and below: Two delightful scenes from Blackford Bridge Congregational Church's coronation pageant, 1911. The little lads must have lapped up the chance of honouring the Sailor King, George V, by dressing as jolly tars, and as for the girls, even the Whit Walks must have paled into insignificance after this spectacular.

The sun shines bright and the floral carpet cuts a colourful swathe along Market Street as the recently crowned King George V and Queen Mary walk away from the platform outside the Derby Hotel during their royal visit in July 1913. Little children, and chambermaids in white aprons, enjoy a better view of the proceedings than most of their fellow citizens from the lower windows of the hotel. It was the first visit of a reigning monarch to Bury, and the streets were thronged with crowds from the royal couple's entry into the town at Heap Bridge to their departure via Knowsley Street and Manchester Road (see overleaf).

King George and Queen Mary were in town, but for the crowds waiting to cheer them in Knowsley Street in July 1913 there were plenty of reminders of more mundane, everyday life—the abattoirs behind the hoardings, and advertisements for the likes of Colman's and Robin Starch, Panshine and Oxo. This being the approach to the railway station, there are also posters for holidays in Wales, on Loch Lomond and in Great Western Railway country, as well as for the more accessible delights of a brass band contest and a Balkan War pageant at Belle Vue, the big pleasure grounds in south Manchester.

Opposite above: Bury to Belgium is the message on the lorry, and it's a reminder that the clothes-to-Eastern-Europe campaigns of the early 1990s had a precedent back in 1914. The Germans invaded Belgium in that year, and it was the brainwave of Arthur Ashworth, who ran a chemical works at Fernhill, to launch an appeal for clothing and bedding for the victims. This first load, weighing 15 cwt, went off in the September via the Belgian consul in London. The sacks are adorned with the flags of the two nations, along with illustrations of hands clasped in friendship.

Below: This tank would scarcely have had Kaiser Bill quaking in his spiked helmet, since it was no more than a wooden mock-up. All communities donated to the war effort and come May 1919 the government felt it was time that they were rewarded for their patriotism. Large cities received real tanks, which, in truth, they didn't know what to do with. The likes of Bury ended up with these cunning imitations, which had the bonus of being almost entirely biodegradable. After posing with the mayor, this one was consigned to a quiet corner of Manchester Road Park where over the years, like all old soldiers, it simply faded away.

Above and below: When the Prince of Wales looked in on Bury on a glorious July day in 1921, it was inevitable that veterans of the Great War should command his attention before luncheon in the Derby Hall with Lord Derby and civic dignitaries.

Above and below: The scene around the Derby Hall gives some idea of the excitement generated by the Prince's visit. No local authority spending on decorations, the future Edward VIII had ordered, but of course decorations there were, and no more so than on the Bury Coffee Rooms, to the right of the bottom picture. The Coffee Rooms' efforts to mark his grandfather's coronation, nineteen years earlier, are recalled on page 42.

Focal point of the Whit Walks was Union Square, seen here just before the Second World War.

Opposite above: No royalty this time, but the opening of the Co-Op Milk Depot in Georgiana Street, on a grey day in 1927, drew a modest crowd of mainly elderly men.

Opposite below: While nobody could possibly wish to live in any other town than Bury, it has always been nice to get away for a while. The tyres of this Vulcan chara look hard, and what's the betting the hood leaks, but these members of Blackford Bridge Congregational Church still look as if they are relishing the prospect of their trip.

Above and below: Coronation, 1953, and Warth Mills put out the flags. See also our picture on page 30.

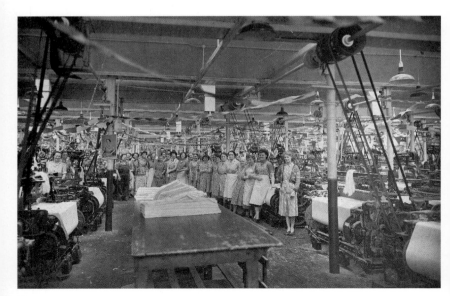

Above and below: Memories of Blackford Bridge Congregational Church in the immediate post-war years; above, the first choir trip after the hostilities, 1946, and below, the adult class processes up Blackford Brow past the golf club entrance on its Whit Walk, c. 1950.

Three cheers for the young Queen on her visit to Bury with the Duke of Edinburgh on 22 October, 1954, less than three years after her accession to the throne. She drew huge crowds, and her peacock-blue outfit was much admired by the throngs lining her route from Bury to Manchester.

Not quite so august an occasion, but the Duke of Edinburgh was a popular return visitor when he unveiled a plaque at Bury Grammar School in November 1976 to commemorate the 250th anniversary of its refoundation by Roger Kay.

Four

Pubs and Picture Palaces

Most who remember the Royal Cinema at the corner of Princess Street and Market Street recall a sleek art deco building, but the cream tiles merely disguised this ornate façade. Opened for the Christmas panto of 1889, and apparently completed only seconds before curtains-up, the Theatre Royal Opera House was the work of James Byrom of Woolfold, a respected joiner, builder and brickmaker whose contracts around that time ranged from everything from railway bridges for the LYR to the British stand at the Brussels Exhibition. The Royal became a cinema in 1933 and, for the compiler at least, for some intangible reason it became the favourite picture house in Bury. Happy memories from around 1960 include four viewings of *A Kind Of Loving*, part of which was filmed in Radcliffe, and a live show starring Adam Faith.

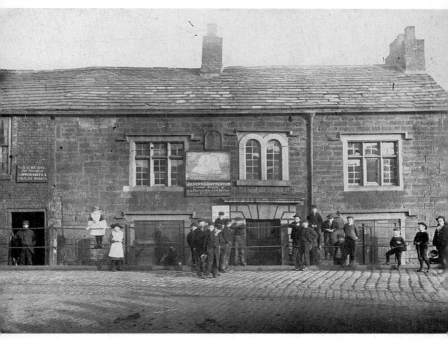

Now here was a low boozer, the Ship Inn at Bury Bridge. The landlord at this time was Joe Chatterton, but there seems to be no sign of him or his customers here, the picture having been hijacked by the local youngsters. On the left, at the doorway of his workshop, is Hayhurst, the coppersmith and tinplate worker. This part of town, at the bottom of Bolton Street, has been changed beyond recognition by roadworks, but the poor old Ship Inn did not even live long enough to see the motor age. It was demolished in 1884, and the Elton Picture House was later built on the site.

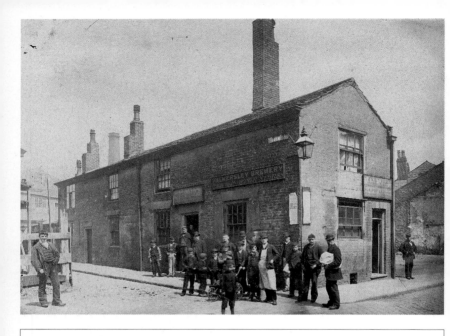

The Edenfield horse-bus is crowded as it passes the Hark to Towler on Walmersley Road at Limefield. Pubs commemorating the deeds of hunting hounds—a celebrated Towler ran with the Holcombe in Victorian times—were common in the North in the nineteenth century.

Opposite above: The Fox Inn in Eden Street, off the Rock, c. 1890. John Wild, the landlord, did not have to go far to restock, since the pub was next door to Bob Chadwick's Walmersley Brewery.

Opposite below: Later memories of the Scala in its cinema days were of a forlorn island of dreams amid the razed wastelands of the Mosses. Now Spring Street is once more a cen
tre of commercial life and the Scala lives on, albeit as a snooker hall.

No picture house in Bury had a greater sense of occasion than the Circus Varieties, standing opposite the Art Picture House on the site of the old open market and today's Metro bus station. A product of those pioneering days of cinema when short films were used simply to supplement live entertainment, it was demolished just as the industry was taking off, in 1916.

Opposite above: Neighbouring pubs at the junction of Parkhills Road and Manchester Road—the Pack Horse and Staff of Life. Too close for comfort? Apparently not, since both are still trading today.

Opposite below: A proud Charlie Broadbent stands at the door of his Bridge Inn at Blackford Bridge, while the regulars give him moral support from the bay window. No wonder he looks pleased with himself, for in this picture his pub looks like an advertisement for the bricklayer's craft. Such a solid looking building, but sadly, a gas explosion in the 1990s reduced to rubble.

Church Street, and on the right the Star Cinema, a picture house serving the teeming little streets of the north end of town. The cinema still stands, having been used most recently for light engineering, and in the brickwork on its Wash Lane gable end can still be read the words 'Twice Nightly, Matinees Monday and Tuesday, Children's Matinees Every Saturday'. The houses of Church Street have been replaced by modern ones built to a similar scale, but the intersecting Brick Street survives, as does St Paul's church, which dates from the early 1840s.

Bury Palais was quite a place. Julie Goodyear of Coronation Street recalls singing there and having a meat pie thrown at her, and the only wonder was that there was not a half brick in it. When they put up a sign saying 'Youths In Edwardian Dress Not Admitted' in the teddy boy era it was like putting up a sign outside Heaven saying 'No Angels'. They who live by the sword die by the sword, however, and this is the sad sight on the last day of the Palais, which went up in smoke just about the time Elvis was giving way to The Beatles.

Five

Military Matters

Lancashire Rifles officers, c. 1880.

Lancashire Fusiliers officers around the time of the Boer War, c. 1898. Wellington Barracks on Bolton Road were built before the Crimean War, and served as the headquarters of the regiment that was to become the Fusiliers, barring more general wartime use, from 1873 to 1970.

A young Bury lad, now every inch a Lancashire Fusilier, bids farewell to his mother in late Victorian times. No doubt the picture was meant as a recruiting tool, but mum has the look of resigned apprehension that has been worn by her kind for as long as old men have used young men to fight their wars.

Marching as to war: Lancashire Fusiliers Volunteers parade to the parish church before sailing for the Boer War. Many of the regiment died at Spion Kop, the hill whose name was later applied, with wry northern humour, to the towering open terraces of several major football grounds.

Reservists report for duty in the Boer War at Wellington Barracks, 1899.

After the bloody war it was back to pomp and circumstance when the Drill Hall was extended in the early years of the twentieth century. The foundation stone was laid by the Fusiliers' 1st Volunteer Battalion CO in 1906, and the extension was opened by the Duke of Connaught in the following year. Along with the original building, built on the site of Bury Castle in around 1870, it still serves the town in a variety of ways.

Above and below: Local lads, the Bury Bantams, reporting for duty early in the First World War, in which many were to die at Gallipoli.

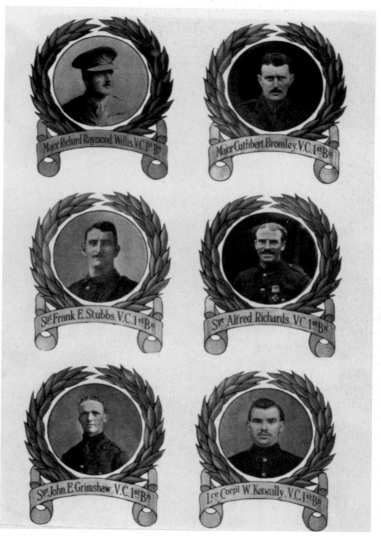

Major Richard Raymond Willis V.C. 1st Bn

Major Cuthbert Bromley V.C. 1st Bn

Sgt Frank E. Stubbs V.C. 1st Bn

Sgt Alfred Richards V.C. 1st Bn

Sgt John E. Grimshaw V.C. 1st Bn

Lce Corpl W. Keneally V.C. 1st Bn

While Gallipoli was a disaster for the Lancashire Fusiliers, the heroism shown in the battle became legendary in the regiment, which remained forever proud of its 'six VCs before breakfast'. Here they are honoured in a recruiting poster produced shortly after the Great War.

With memories of the war still painfully recent, Fusiliers march to the parish church on Gallipoli Sunday, April 1923. Taking the salute, bottom right, are CO Colonel Needham and the Mayor, Councillor Redford.

Above and right: Wellington Barracks are returned to the Lancashire Fusiliers as their training depot after more general wartime use in 1951. Above, the first draft bash the square once more, while on the right, standing guard at the war memorial on Bolton Road, are two soldiers, one dressed in modern uniform and the other in that worn at the Battle of Minden, a Seven Years War encounter in 1759. Like Gallipoli, Minden was deeply embedded in the lore of the regiment, a day when the 20th Foot, the Fusiliers' predecessors, put the French cavalry to flight.

Fusiliers officers celebrate Minden Day during the Second World War, wearing roses in their caps. According to lore, the Battle of Minden saw the 20th Foot and other regiments of redcoats pass through gardens on their way to take on the French cavalry and their heavy guns, and as they did so they picked roses and stuck them in their caps. Though the blooms in this picture appear to be a light colour, Lancashire's affinity with the red rose no doubt helped to strengthen this tradition.

Gallipoli Sunday 1990, the 75th anniversary of the battle, and there was still a living link with that fateful day in the proud figure of Bob Spencer, on the left. Keeping him company was Benny Adams, a Manchester Regiment veteran who was also there that day, having faked his age and joined up at fourteen.

Above: Smart turn-out: a vintage photograph of Bury Grammar School's cadet corps.

Left: Still on parade: the Duke of Edinburgh inspects the school's CCF during his visit in November 1976.

Six

On the Fringes

Not such a pretty scene as the ones opposite. Limefield Mill and Cottages at Pigslee Brow to the north of the town are a reminder that perhaps the good old days were not all that great, after all. This is just one recollection among several in this book of the wretched housing conditions inflicted on so many of our forefathers in the years when cotton was king.

Opposite, above and below: Edwardian pleasure grounds. Walmersley Road Recreation Ground was all things to all men, women and children in the days when such amenities were an integral part of life—a playground for the little ones, a family day out when the bands were oompahing on Sunday afternoons, a monkey run for the teenagers on warm summer Sunday evenings ...

A mucky Rochdale Old Road at Huntley Brook, just below the old weavers' cottages on page 34. The tallest of the group of children outside Hoyle's shop seems to be wearing a straw hat. In fact it is a youth with a shopping basket on his head, the handle under his chin, proving the point that daft Bury lads have been with us a long time.

A boring new council housing estate in 1937, or one of the most fascinating pictures in this book? The compiler tends towards the latter point of view for, while the houses on Ferngrove West and Kingfisher Drive on Chesham's 'Dickie Bird Estate' remain superficially unaltered, the M66 now roars along an embankment above the wasteland in the foreground. A concrete underpass very close to where the horse is standing leads to Ferngrove East and the estate's three 'Finches' Drives.

Above and below: The Infirmary, now the General Hospital, opened in Walmersley Road in 1882. The picture above was taken some eighteen years later. The children's ward, below, followed in 1923, opened by Lord Derby in memory of Bury men who died in the First World War.

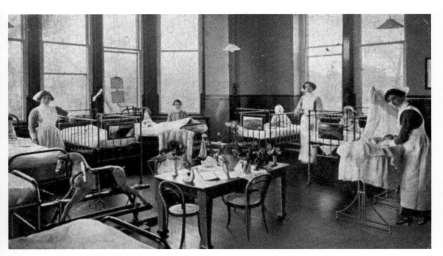

Blackford Bridge in 1890, when the Congregational Church was newly opened, the foundation stone having been laid in 1888. Woodley Terrace was built on the field to the right of the church in 1898. The bridge across the Roch was rebuilt in 1904, though the ruins of a far more ancient structure stand slightly down river. The children standing in the farm garden are Nellie and Rachel Rigby.

Almost like a day by the sea: you could always escape to Elton Reservoir.

Seven

The Shopping Streets

The kind of scene that made the artist L.S. Lowry tick: Bury between the wars, with Union Square punctuating the streets of mills and terraced houses.

Opposite above: Whitehead Gardens, between Knowsley Street and Manchester Road, in the 1920s, after the Fusiliers' Boer War memorial had been moved from the Market Place, but some years before the new Town Hall sprang up on the brow of the hill in the mid-1930s. The clock tower was built in white Portland stone, in 1914, by Henry Whitehead. He was the benefactor who created the gardens from the grounds of a former private lunatic asylum, in memory of his surgeon brother Walter, a former president of the British Medical Association.

Opposite below: The object of morbid curiosity for generations of little Bury boys, the abattoirs off Knowsley Street lasted for seventy years, from 1902 to 1972. The site now forms part of the Metro interchange.

Carr's of Knowsley Street was best known by most people in Bury for its chara trips—a far cry from the chauffeur-driven limousine and accompanying nobs used to advertise their cars.

The more usual face of motor travel at Carr's, at least for the average citizen c. 1920. Here, charas registered EN 1316 and EN 1258 carry contrasting groups of passengers—women and young children on the left, and big lads in caps (one with an arm in a sling) in the balloon-bedecked vehicle to the rear.

You can almost smell the celery, black puddings and Uncle Joe's Mint Balls: the Moss Street flank of the market in the mid-1960s.

Bury Market, covered and open, shortly before the disastrous fire of 1968. To the right in Market Street are the Queen's Hotel and Co-Op Emporium.

And this is how it all ended: the blaze that gutted the market hall in November 1968.

Opposite above: No coming back. The cold light of day reveals the full extent of the damage to the covered market.

Opposite below: On the site of Kay Gardens, Lord Derby's Market operated from 1839 to 1901, when the covered market that was destroyed in the 1968 fire was opened. At the time of this picture it was in its final days, for posters around the doorway tell of the new market on the fairground. A group of women in shawls are gossiping beside Berry's florists, to the right of a stall advertising Victory Gums. Derby's butchers is the stall on the right, and both they and Berry's were granted prominent roadside positions in the new market.

The tramway centre in Haymarket Street beside Kay Gardens, 1936. The first tram was destined for Blackford Bridge and the second for Radcliffe. The Co-Op with its Emporium Restaurant stands beyond the Kay Memorial to the right.

Opposite above: Miss Mary Cooper owned this tearoom on the market but, because of her initials, she was Ma Cooper to thousands. Teacakes and meatpies are prominent in her window display, along with a colourful advertisement for Crawford's biscuits. The prices on the bill of fare to the left are unfortunately not legible.

Opposite below: Kay Gardens and the old covered market, 1955. The gardens were created between 1907 and 1908, and the bill for laying them out was again met by Henry Whitehead (see page 87). The central memorial is to John Kay, one of Bury's most famous sons as the inventor of the flying shuttle and an ancestor of Whitehead.

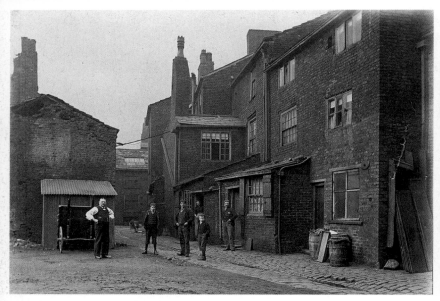

One of our occasional reminders that it could be a mean old town in the years before the First World War. This was Back Fleet Street, but it could have been any number of inner-town alleyways.

Now partly buried beneath the Mill Gate Shopping Centre, Haymarket Street crossed Market Street to become one of the three sides of Kay Gardens. On the right in this scene from around 1960, Sly's jewellers and Morris's wallpaper shop are familiar names - as, on the corner of Broad Street (centre of picture), is the late lamented UCP tripe shop and café. Tripe and onions, steak and cowheels—it's a sad old world in which you can't move for pizzas and hamburgers but won't find delicacies like those for love or money.

The Garrick's Head on the corner of Spring Street and Princess Street looks like a corner pub as ever was, but there's change in the air in the 1950s. The dress and the shiny car are almost symbols of the decade, and even if motoring was still a little beyond your reach you could buy a bike by weekly payments from Frank Aspinall.

Opposite: Silver Street in the 1950s. The weather was nasty and it was probably early closing day. It doesn't sound the most promising formula for a photograph, yet this picture is surely one of the most appealing in the book.

Mirror image. The looking-glass above Sam Count's shop in Silver Street reflects passers-by and attracts their attention to the flag-bedecked portrait of the future Edward VII and Queen Alexandra. The Prince of Wales Feathers are on the shield to the right. The royal wedding, perhaps? If so, it makes this picture one of the oldest in this collection, for that takes us back to 1863.

W.A. Duckworth started off on Bury Market, but by the 1890s he was one of the leading fish and fruit merchants in town at 9 Silver Street. An arch-rival of Peter Hardman in Fleet Street, he took special pride in beating him to the early season fruits and put on an astonishing display of turkeys, geese and ducks at Christmas.

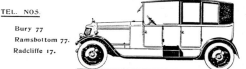

Central Carriage Company Limited,

BURY.

"YES, IT'S TRUE,"

The Central Carriage Company Ltd. have the Finest Fleet of Motors . in the District, and are now booking them up for Weddings. .

TEL. NOS.

Bury 77.
Ramsbottom 77.
Radcliffe 17.

AGENTS for the
STANDARD CAR

Spares kept in
Stock.

Come and Inspect our Cars before placing your order elsewhere as we make a Speciality of Weddings. We never fail to finish the work we undertake as we have the Cars and the Men.

Why not have a Private Car without a Hackney Carriage Plate stuck on the back, for Shopping and Weddings, then it will look like your own Car?

WEDDINGS FROM £1·0·0

Silver Street was also the home of the Co-Op carriage and motor depot. Didn't they show a grasp of human nature with their 'Why not have a Private Car without a Hackney Carriage Plate stuck on the back—then it will look like your own Car?'

A sunny morning outside the Royal Hotel, Silver Street, c. 1890.

The ACTIVE MAN.

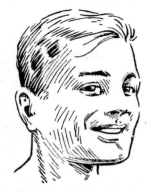

Be moderate in all things. No one knows the truth of that better than the Active Man. Too much smoking or too heavy a meal may easily result in losing the match. That is why the Active Man *who knows* enjoys a dainty dish of Tripe or Cowheels before games. As nutritious as red meat, far more easily digested and far more economical, they are essentially an ideal food for men of energy. But there is Tripe— and TRIPE ; Cowheels—and COWHEELS. Be sure it is U.C.P. Tripe (9d. per lb.) and Cowheels (3d. per lb.) which is your guarantee of superfine Quality, Absolute Purity, and Daily Freshness. They can only be purchased at those shops where the U.C.P. oval red sign is displayed. *Buy where you see this Sign.*

TRIPE AND U C LTD P COWHEELS

JOHN COX, King St., BURY.
(Branch of the United Cattle Products Ltd.)

A HOUSEHOLD TREASURE :—

Have you yet got your copy of the U.C.P. "99 Recipe Book" which contains many nutritious, appetising and economical methods of enjoying more, frequently U.C.P. Tripe and Cowheel.

Make a purchase to-day at any shop displaying the U.C.P. Oval Red Sign, and ask for your free copy.

THE SIGN OF PURITY & QUALITY

PURITY U C LTD P QUALITY

this shop is supplied with

TRIPE AND COWHEELS
FRESH DAILY

Branch of UNITED CATTLE PRODUCTS LTD.

BUY ONLY WHERE YOU SEE THIS OVAL RED SIGN.

C 5·1

You didn't believe the unsolicited testimonial to UCP products on page 95? You'll believe it now ...

From the year in which Dickens published Bleak House, 1852, this is the earliest known photograph of Bury. It tells us much about life in this other world more than 150 years ago. They had buses that ran to Whitefield, fly posters stuck up bills advertising cough cures and Chatwood safes, and John Whittaker had no qualms about hanging his poultry beside the muck and rubble of the building work at Sparrow and Pearn's tailors shop. You could also stand in the middle of the Market Place without a motor bus making a ghost of you, even if the camera did.

Steam trams began operating in March 1883, with a service to Blackford Bridge and beyond. The destinations flagged up on the boards of this one in the Market Place are Higher Broughton, Prestwich, Whitefield and Bury.

Looking down Bolton Street from the Market Place in the late nineteenth century, the most notable buildings are the Coffee Rooms on the left and Driffield's big drapers shop on the right.

Opposite above : The Two Tubs in the Wylde in one of its mock-Tudor reincarnations at around the turn of the twentieth century. Though it is still officially the Globe Inn, its nickname dates from the 1830s when members of the Toasted Cheese Club who met there decided it needed a new sign. A member called Shaw hit on the idea of cutting a barrel in two and putting the halves up together on the wall to represent the two hemispheres. If you think about it, the two tubs can be made to represent a rough-and-ready globe.

Opposite below: A steam tram at the end of Market Street outside the Derby Hotel. The loss of the Derby to indifferent modern redevelopment was another act of 'brave new world' change that many have come to regret; indeed, many regretted it at the time, in 1965. Designed by Sydney Smirke, an architect of national repute, the Derby opened in 1850 as part of a classical hotel and town hall development commissioned by Lord Derby, along with the accompanying Derby Hall and Athenaeum.

Above: A close-up of the scene on the previous page, this time with the Clarence Hotel hoving into view at the junction of Silver Street and Bolton Street.

Left: So many specialist shops for collars and spats, stockings and ties. For people with money to spare in late Victorian Britain there was little to spend it on beyond clothes and things for the home. This stylish little art deco logo was used in the 1920s to advertise Ambler's the hatters, a Bolton Street business founded in 1891.

Above and below: Two views of a part of Bolton Street now swept away completely by the inner ring road roundabout. Above, the portrait of a lady advertises Robinson's, whose Water Street shops are recalled on page 20. Other advertisements are for Heap and Son's tailors in Rock Street, Bradbury bicycles, Wheatley's beer, the Ramsbottom Annual Show and Keating's Powder, the bug and flea deterrent that really needed no advertising in turn-of-the-century Bury. Below is T. Howard's furnishing and general store.

Above and below: Two memories of the chain of dry-cleaning shops built up in the inter-war years by the Allen family. Above, the clean-cut image of the 1950s at the Union Street branch; left, Clifford Allen at the Bridge Street, Ramsbottom shop before the war. The special offer of cleaning for 2s. 9d., a tenth of many people's weekly wage, is a reminder that having your clothes cleaned was an undertaking not to be taken lightly. The company lives on with two branches, at Georgiana Street and in Rochdale.

Above, below left and below right: No doubt many people loved Union Square—it certainly served as a happy reminder of Whit Walks—but by the 1950s it struck many others as a dreary anachronism, and it is hard to argue that the modern shopping centre that has taken its place does not represent an improvement in the quality of life. One aspect of the square that is still mourned is the passing of Casewell's black pudding shop (below) which closed in 1968. Owned latterly by Vincent Ashworth, its history went back to the early nineteenth century, and it claimed its product was the original Bury pudding. More high-profile by far was Thompson's stall on Bury Market, run from pre-war days until his death in 1971 by the ever-cheery Harry Reddish.

The ONLY ADDRESS in the
World where the Original
BURY PUDDINGS
are made
CASEWELL'S
60 UNION STREET, BURY.   Tel. 1953
Established over 130 years

Rain, mackintoshes and hoods—but what wouldn't you give to return to the Bury of the early 1950s for an hour or so, to remind yourself of all that's gone? This is Tithebarn Street at its junction with the Rock in late summer. The 'What's On' posters advertise the Star, Regal, Royal, Scala and Art Cinemas. The latter was showing On The Town, with Gene Kelly and Frank Sinatra. At Gigg Lane, Bury are about to entertain Birmingham in the Second Division, a league they never descended beneath until 1957.

Eight

The Happiest Days
of Their Lives

Junior Bury Grammar School boys in the 1880s, when their schoolmaster was the Revd E.J.S. Lamburn, who taught there from 1876 to 1915. He is best remembered as the father of Richmal Crompton, the Bury-born author of the Just William books, and her brother John, who as John Lambourne wrote several books on natural history. As John is also thought to have been his sister's chief source of inspiration for her stories, it could be said that the unsmiling young man seen here is none other than William Brown's dad. Local names abound in the list of pupils in this picture—all the young Haworths, Nuttalls, Jopsons, Boltons, Cromptons, Hursts and Inghams.

Opposite above: A schoolroom in the old Bury Grammar School in the Wylde, with Latin declensions on the blackboard and a map of old Ireland on the wall. As for the object descending from the ceiling, the imaginative might almost believe it was an instrument of torture amid such cheerless surroundings.

Opposite below: Lord Stanley, Lord Derby's son, lays the foundation stone of the new grammar school assembly hall, part of the buildings now occupied by Bury Grammar School for Girls, in June 1906. The £4,000 cost of the hall was again met by Henry Whitehead (see pages 87 and 92); and as both he and Lord Stanley were Freemasons, the stone was laid 'plumb, level and square' with full Masonic pomp. The hall was opened by Lady Stanley early the following year. The boys' school moved to this site in 1903, the girls following just months before this picture was taken *(see page 116).*

Fourth form, Bury Grammar School, 1912, with form master A.J. Nicholas giving the impression that he is perhaps trying to look older and sterner than he was in real life. Familiar local names again abound among the pupils—Nuttall, Crompton, Greenhalgh, Barlow and Clegg.

The remove, Bury Grammar School, 1919-20. Isn't there always somebody like the little fellow crouching on the right, turning a scene of relative dignity and repose into near farce?

Above: Eton collars look clean and starched in this Bury Grammar School form of around 1912.

Below: The first Bury Grammar School for Girls, founded in 1884 in Bolton Street as the Girls' High School. It moved to share the boys' school premises it now occupies solely in January 1906, when its official opening ceremony was the first of two visits that year by Lord Stanley (see page 112).

Above and below: Bury Grammar School for Girls memories of 1909. Above, a staff group; below, Form III Lower surrounding their form mistress and headmistress. The head was well known beyond the playground walls: Jane Kitchener, a cousin of the First World War Field Marshal and war minister immortalized by the poster 'Your Country Needs You'. She was the school's founding principal and was the longest-serving headmistress in England when she retired after thirty-six years, shortly after the Armistice.

Bury Grammar School for Girls' Kindergarten and Form I, 1911. How did they keep those dresses clean? Have little girls really changed so much?

Opposite above: No buttons and bows here: a crocodile of Bury Grammar schoolgirls, early 1950s.

Opposite below: The headmistress and staff of Bury Grammar School for Girls, 1954.

The day we met the Duke: Prince Philip with Grammar School Girls, November 1976.

Infants' drill at Bury Convent Preparatory School, 1910.

All is orderly in these classroom scenes from Bury Convent High School in 1909, above, and 1907, opposite.

Junior pupils in the convent lab, c. 1935: who said girls never did science?

The procession for the crowning of the statue of the Virgin Mary, Bury Convent, 1948.

Dancing on the lawn, Bury Convent, July 1954.

The opening of the new Bury Convent High School building, now Holy Cross College, performed by the Bishop of Salford, April 1952.

Nine

This Sporting Life

Bury Football Club was never more a force in the land than in 1903, when their 6–0 victory over Derby County in the FA Cup Final at Crystal Palace created a record final score still unsurpassed to this day. It made their 4–0 win over Southampton in the first final of the century, three years previously, seem almost an underachievement in comparison. The men who delivered the goods against Derby were, standing, left to right: Johnston, Lindsay, Thorpe, Monteith, McEwan and Ross; seated: Richards, Wood, Sagar, Leeming and Plant.

These are the players who returned Bury to the first division in 1924 and hauled them to fourth in the table, the club's highest ever position in the league, two years later. The team boasted international players in Ball, Bullock and Bradshaw, but perhaps best remembered by old-timers today are its dashing wingers, Amos and Robbie. The club lost its first division status in 1929, and is taking rather a long time to regain it.

Pre-season training at Lower Gigg Lane, August 1960. By April 1961 Bury had amassed more goals and points than at any time before or since and, in finishing top of the third division, landed their first of two championships of the twentieth century, the other being in 1997. Even today, scores of misty-eyed fifty-something men in Bury will reel off with pride the names of Adams, Robertson, Conroy, Turner, McGrath, Atherton, Calder, Holden, Watson, Jackson and Hubbard.

Left: In the days of heavy-handed sporting cartoons the Bury Shakers were inevitably portrayed as shivering undertakers. This one is from an Everton programme of the early 1950s, decades after undertakers had ceased to wear toppers draped in black crepe.

Opposite: There have been times when Bury FC has not marketed itself as well as it might. The Shakers player on the cover of this programme from 1937 is the prancing ninny on the right, appearing as if he is about to strike his poised, purposeful-looking opponent with his handbag.

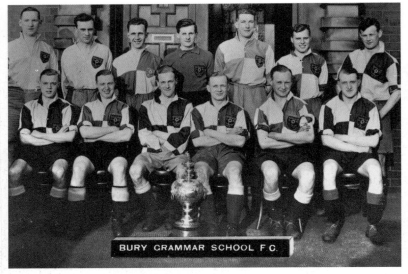

BURY GRAMMAR SCHOOL F.C.

A true curio, this Ardath cigarette card of the 1930s features Bury Grammar School Old Boys' Football Club, no less. The reverse solemnly records that the lads won the northern section of the Lancashire Amateur League in 1932 and 1936, and lists all the players. Goalkeeper Frank Oldroyd went on to become the Old Boys' Association President.

Athletics in the nineteenth century: the start of a two-mile scratch race at the Bury Cricket Club ground, 1896.

Bury lad Reg Harris became famous for racing at the cambered cycle track at Fallowfield in south Manchester. By the early 1950s the town had a cycledrome of its own, the Ashworth track on wasteland near Pilot Mill at the bottom of Alfred Street. There appears to be a good turnout for this meeting in 1952 but, in spite of this, the venture never really got off the ground.

Bury Water Polo Club, captained by S. Cheetham, in 1896. W. Nuttall, seated to his right, was a swimming instructor who died at Gallipoli nineteen years later.

Was that a cockroach in the water, or something worse? Bury Baths were opened as early as 1864, and those who remember using them a century later recall all kinds of horror stories, most of them probably apocryphal. Changing was on two tiers in private cubicles around the pool, and those who feel that the modern open-plan approach to changing is an improvement on this have obviously never had to change with a class of thirty eleven-year-olds dashing around them.

Right and below: Nellie Halstead was a cheery Bury Athletics Club star who represented Great Britain in the Women's World Games in 1930 and was the British champion at 100, 220 and 440 yards the following year. She was the first of a number of outstanding women athletes to represent the club that decade

Opposite: Betjeman might have written a poem in praise of them: Bury Grammar School's Alice Crompton and Phyllis Whittle, Lancashire Girls' Schools tennis champions, 1927.

Above: Bury Athletics Club athletes and cyclist co-members, 1930s.

Below: All on a summer's day. Bury Athletics Club members line up for a race in the 1930s.

Another Bury Athletics Club star of the 1930s, Hilda Hodson.

Bury Athletics Club Women's Relay Team, which won the Northern Women's Championships in 1930.

Above: Bury boy Reg Harris, seen in the foreground here at his peak in the early 1950s, became a world champion racing cyclist—and then made a remarkable comeback when well into middle age.

Left: A man who rose to the top in sports administration in both cycling and athletics was Bury businessman Dick Taylor. He was an official for the British cycling team at the 1948 Olympics in London, an international timekeeper in athletics and national chairman of the Women's AAA from 1938 to 1969. Shortly before his retirement from that post he presented a perpetual trophy to be contested by WAAA members.

Opposite, above and below: Bury Athletics Club memories of 1927. Above, the team that won the East Lancashire junior cross-country championships; below, cheerful faces at the start of a road race.

Bury Athletics Club youngsters with coaches (both athletics and motor), 1930.

With scarcely a crash helmet in sight, members of Bury Motor Club line up beside Kay Gardens in Moss Street at the start of a rally in 1921. A few of the motorcycles have side-cars, but the great craze for them had not yet arrived. Almost every number-plate on view is EN followed by four digits, a reminder of just how tight-knit a world it was in the Bury of eighty-plus years ago, when even a Salford or Bolton number-plate would have made you stand out from the crowd. Landmarks on the row of Haymarket Street properties to the rear include the Knowsley and Rayner's Vaults pubs.

Above: A top athlete in Bury in the 1960s was Vivien Flett, a sprinter and long-jumper, seen here displaying her technique to young Bury Athletics Club members in the gym.

Left: In 1963 it seemed a good idea to call in ballet teacher Pat Lupino to teach some of Bury's young athletes dance exercises. At least the lads seem happy enough with this leaping and stretching routine.

Bury Athletics Club women hosted the 1964 national cross-country championships at Elton School, and were not too busy organizing the event to neglect winning it. Their four counters, seen here with the handsome shield, were, left to right: Lesley Helliwell, Joyce Ashcroft, Brenda Bailey and Kath Hudson.

Left: Bury Athletics Club's best-known name in a big decade for its women, the 1960s, was Morecambe schoolgirl Mary Hodson, seen here in her Olympic year of 1964.

Below: Bury Athletics Club members get together for a dance in Heywood in 1967, and welcome the New Zealand runner Mollie Sampson, centre, as a guest. From left to right are Mrs R. Knowles, Terry Ratcliffe, Oliver Knowles and Mary Hodson.

Mary Hodson did not return from the Olympics in Tokyo with a medal, but she celebrated her eighteenth birthday there, and her memories of the games will never fade. Here she is seen in her 800 metres heat battling it out with Kraan of the Netherlands.

Sweet and genteel maidens, until it came to playing hockey. In 1908–9 the Bury Grammar School for Girls team played and won eight games, scored fifty-two goals and conceded just one. Their scores included an 11–0, a 10–0 and two 8–0s, and they rewarded Bella Vista, who scored the season's only goal against them, by putting six past their goalie. They saw off Bury Ladies 2–0, and their biggest scare of the season was when Oldham Grammar School restricted them to a single goal. Captain M. Hardman is seen next to their games mistress, with the ball.

Ten

Meet the Folks

The first choir at Bury parish church with choirmaster E.J. Sparke, c. 1860.

The Revd Hugh Hornby with the parish church choir, 1936.

One last get-together before the war: past pupils of Bury Convent, 1939.

Smart men, smart sound: Warth Prize Brass Band.

Above: Triangles, drums and tambourines: Bury Convent Prep School's percussion band in 1933.

Opposite above: Billy Allen went on to become a local dry-cleaning magnate and a sometimes controversial chairman of Bury Football Club, but there was a time in his youth when all that seemed to matter most was the next gig with his Lyricals at Raffertys on the Rock. His brother Arnold was also in the line-up of this syncopating combo.

Opposite below: ot much syncopation here, one suspects. The Tenterden Street Baptist Church Orchestra is seen here under its conductor, Mr Kay, who let his spirit soar with fine music at the end of working days at Kay and Wilkinson's leather works in Butcher Lane.

Above: A turn-of-the-century picture of the family of Colonel O.O. Walker of Chesham House, whose four daughters never married and became well known in the town, driving in their open carriage to the shops or church until the last one died in 1955. Colonel Walker was a mayor of Bury and high sheriff of Lancashire. The house, empty after the death of the last Miss Walker, was quickly vandalized and eventually demolished.

Above: They didn't inspire a TV series set in Holmfirth, did they? Affectionately remembered Bury Athletics Club stalwarts, Jack Brown, George Goddard and Eddie Leeming.

Right: Portrait of a gentleman: an example of the work of Edmund Eccles, a Victorian artist and photographer of Broad Street. Apart from specializing in visiting cards such as this, he turned his hand to enlarging portraits up to life size and having them coloured in oils, water-colours or chalk.

Opposite, below left: Just like a film star: Miss Bury, Winifred Forkin, Cotton Queen 1934–5.

Opposite, below right: There was not a picture house in town with a greater sense of occasion than the Art, and if its art deco Compion organ were to be auctioned today, it would doubtless sell for more than the cinema cost to build. A familiar figure at the organ in the inter-war years was Frank Melia, a true musical showman behind those studious spectacles.

Members of the 44th Bury Scouts, founded as the Rector of Bury's Own Troop in the inter-war years by a curate at the parish church.

Right: The Revd Ralph Wilson, founder of the 44th Bury troop and a former curate at the parish church.

Below: Long after his departure, the 44th Bury troop honoured their founder by naming their new HQ the Wilson Hall, after him.

Who says it's all dark satanic mills? Bury Scouts and Guides indulge in what has been one of their favourite occupations for generations—escaping down the road to the abidingly lovely Ashworth Valley.

Acknowledgements

Thanks for the loan of pictures, background information and other help are due to:

Peter Allen • Auty & Lees Ltd • Joan Bowles • Bury Grammar School • Bury Grammar School for Girls • Bury Metro Libraries • The Bury Times • John Carter • Janet Cheetham Peter Cole • Peter Cullen • Vera Duerdin • E. Ellison • G.B. Ellison • Holy Cross College Rita Hirst • the late Mary Hudson • Tony Jowett • Norah Kennedy Rika Kirkpatrick • The Lancashire Fusiliers Museum • Peter Morgan • Lawrence Purcell Edwina Salmon • Graham Simpson • Judith Skinner • the late Canon Reginald Smith Tony Sprason